Penguin Books

The Stick

To Crista...

Michael Leunig

Michael Leunig has been drawing and writing for Australian newspapers since 1965. He was born in Melbourne and now lives on a farm in north-eastern Victoria. *The Stick* comprises pieces that have previously appeared in the Melbourne *Age* and the *Sydney Morning Herald*.

Also by Michael Leunig

The Penguin Leunig
The Second Leunig
The Bedtime Leunig
A Bag of Roosters
Ramming the Shears
The Travelling Leunig
A Common Prayer
The Prayer Tree
Common Prayer Collection
Introspective
A Common Philosophy
Everyday Devils and Angels
A Bunch of Poesy
You and Me
Short Notes from the Long History of Happiness
Why Dogs Sniff Each Other's Tails
Goatperson
The Curly Pyjama Letters
Poems: 1972–2002
Strange Creature
Wild Figments
A New Penguin Leunig

MICHAEL LEUNIG

The Stick

and other tales of our times

PENGUIN BOOKS

PENGUIN BOOKS

Published by the Penguin Group
Penguin Group (Australia)
250 Camberwell Road, Camberwell, Victoria 3124, Australia
(a division of Pearson Australia Group Pty Ltd)
Penguin Group (USA) Inc.
375 Hudson Street, New York, New York 10014, USA
Penguin Group (Canada)
90 Eglinton Avenue East, Suite 700, Toronto ON M4P 2Y3, Canada
(a division of Pearson Penguin Canada Inc.)
Penguin Books Ltd
80 Strand, London WC2R 0RL, England
Penguin Ireland
25 St Stephen's Green, Dublin 2, Ireland
(a division of Penguin Books Ltd)
Penguin Books India Pvt Ltd
11 Community Centre, Panchsheel Park, New Delhi – 110 017, India
Penguin Group (NZ)
Cnr Airborne and Rosedale Roads, Albany, Auckland, New Zealand
(a division of Pearson New Zealand Ltd)
Penguin Books (South Africa) (Pty) Ltd
24 Sturdee Avenue, Rosebank, Johannesburg 2196, South Africa

Penguin Books Ltd, Registered Offices: 80 Strand, London WC2R 0RL, England

First published by Penguin Books Australia Ltd, 2002
This paperback edition published by Penguin Group (Australia), 2006

10 9 8 7 6 5 4 3 2 1

Design by George Dale © Penguin Group (Australia)
Printed and bound in China through Bookbuilders

National Library of Australia
Cataloguing-in-Publication data:

Leunig, Michael, 1945– .
The stick and other tales of our times.
New ed.
ISBN-13: 978 0 14 300146 1.
ISBN-10: 0 14 300146 9.
1. Caricatures and cartoons – Australia. 2. Australian wit and humor, Pictorial. I. Title.
741.5994

www.penguin.com.au

<u>Great uncelebrated inventions — <u>THE STICK</u></u>

The stick was invented in 1272 by Arthur Ernest Augustus Stick, a leech catcher and dealer in Ely, Cambridgeshire, England.

Arthur's original prototype was quite small by modern standards and was used for lifting single leeches from the marshes into earthenware containers.

News of the "stick of Ely" spread quickly and, before long, sticks of all sizes and with various functions became common throughout Europe.

To this day, however, nobody has been able to improve much upon Arthur's humble design — the forked stick being probably the only notable development.

Folding sticks, double sticks and multi-directional sticks are just a few examples of the many variations which have not stood the test of time.

The "stick of Ely" is probably the most common, useful, efficient and enduring invention known to human kind — thanks to Arthur Ernest Augustus Stick of Ely, Cambridgeshire, England.

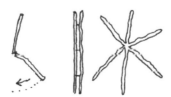

The value of the
soul plunged yesterday
to its lowest level
in five years

one person invested
in a smile

a meteor
plummeted and
a few wishes
were made

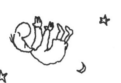

Experts said
nothing

There were rumors
about a small child
who had flown over
the city on a
carpet of rose petals

certain things slid
and crashed but
a cheer rose up
and a dog barked
playfully. A violin
was heard too.

Leunig

PEACE

Peace is my drug.
It stops the pain.
In safe reflecting rooms
Or in a lane
Or in a park
I will lie
And have some peace
And get high.
If it's pure
And there's lots of it about
I overdose
And pass out
And dream of peace:
My favorite thing,
When nobody wants me
And nothing's happening

leunig

It was January when I woke up but it was February before I got out of bed.

By the time I'd had a shower and got dressed it was mid-March.

I had a quick breakfast and tidied up a bit which took until early June.

I scrambled out the door and by the time I got to work it was August.

I made two telephone calls then suddenly I realised it was November.

Oh dear. Now it's December already. Not a scrap of work done. I haven't even read the paper yet!

Leunig

Woes maketh the man;
A troubled heart on a well-cut sleeve,
A well-cut lip, a loose weave,
A sock on the jaw,
A pullover, a fallover on the floor.
A collar well pressed
Against the wall,
Another cuff, another fall,
A good belt, a black tie
A black eye, a huge welt
A felt hat, a hate deeply felt,
A fate with a rip in the rear
A nicely stitched ear
A scarf to match the scar
A scarlet scratch upon the cheek
A splash of crimson from the nose.
Ah yes;
What maketh the man is his woes.

leunig

Welcome to the Club.

Suddenly, unexpectedly, you're in the club.

The club you dreaded. The club you mocked.

It's your turn now. You've joined the club.

And then, around you, you begin to discover others who are also members of the club and you see a sweetness in them that you hadn't seen before.

And you enter into a new world of telltale signs; of gentle knowing looks, little smiles of recognition and fellowship; and you begin to see what a HUGE club this is ...

...what a HUGE, OLD, STEADY, club this is. How tender and deep its wisdom; how quiet its strength; how gracious and consoling its motto,
" RISUS OMNIA — INCRUMENTUS PER DEDECUS — SAPIENTIA PER DAMNUM "
(EVERYTHING IS FUNNY — GROWTH THROUGH HUMILIATION and WISDOM THROUGH LOSS)

leunig

Things in General

Things in general, you'll be pleased to know, are only half as bad as they appear...

...which makes things better by half than otherwise thought...

...or approximately twice as good as we'd imagined

We'd feared that things were probably much worse than we'd dare to contemplate

But if seems we're twice as happy as we'd been prepared to consider; and...

...ten times **as confused**, seven times as ridiculous, four times as funny and twenty-five times as mysterious...

leunig

It is Spring!
The blowfly of love is
on the wing,
Zooming round the ceiling
Where all the paint is peeling.

Above the bed
The blowfly of love rams
its head
Into the light
Then spirals downward
out of sight.

Suddenly it's up!
It somersaults into your cup.
And then it's out again.
It's made it to the window pane!

There! It's on its back,
Spinning like a maniac,
Raging as it dies!
Your heart identifies.

It waits a bit.
Then the blowfly of
love explodes into a fit
Of ballistic, idiotic <u>hell</u>.
You know it well.

You know it will pass.
The blowfly staggers
down the glass.
You know the feeling —
(When all the paint
is peeling.)

Leunig

Everything seems to be dragging on.

Yes but everything seems to be going too fast as well.

What are we talking about?

We're talking about the <u>motion</u> of <u>being</u>.

Is the essential motion of existence a jerking motion?

Yes, for some it is, but for others it's a randomly agitated swirl outwards.

A quick downward dragging hiccupping motion is the way some people feel their life... ...so I'm told.

And yet there are others who just <u>flow</u> with an upside-down flip-flopping looping funny sort of a tumbling glide...

Leunig

I want to be an idiot
And go to idiot land
An idiot bird upon my head
An idiot in my hand

I'd walk like a total idiot
And sing like idiots do
And people would say "what an idiot;
He's an idiot through and through"

And I'd plant an idiot's garden
And live in an idiot's house;
A harmless grinning idiot
With my lovely idiot spouse.

Leunig

The First Day of School. (A SONG) ♪ ♫ ♪

The first day of school could not have been merrier;
The teacher turned out to be a fox terrier
Who taught us to leap and taught us to bark
And chase little birdies all over the park.
For the rest of our lives we still had the spark
From the wonderful first day of school.

leunig

HOW TO HAVE AN OFFICE CHRISTMAS PARTY IF YOU WORK ALONE.
This year's gone fast hasn't it? Amazing!
Hey moth. Merry christmas mate!
Hello. We haven't met before have we? Merry Christmas. You're the blowfly aren't you?
Hey, let's go for a walk or something, just for fun. What do you think? Let's get out of here and get some fresh air.
Spider... SPIDER! Mate. Happy new year mate. Take care. Merry Christmas... Have a good one.
leunig

When your world is feeling stuck
Climb upon a big white duck
Sail away across the dark.
Out towards the little spark

When you reach that tiny star
Put it safely in a jar
Say a prayer and give a quack,
Take it out and put it back;

Put it back and let it be.
Sparkling above the sea,
Above the sea so dark and deep
As you quack yourself to sleep.

leunig

Santa, Santa in your sleigh,
Come and take my toys away
While I'm sleeping in my cot
Visit me and take the lot.

Santa, Santa set me free,
Clear an open space for me;
Me and all the girls and boys
Buried under heaps of toys.

Santa, Santa with your sack,
Come and take some plastic back;
Take it back and in its place,
Leave a little breathing space.

Leunig

Christmas is
like a battered
little suitcase...

which cannot
possibly hold
what is meant
to fit into it.

It comes unstuck.
Things spill out.

... Merry
Suitcase ...

People are like
that too;
Thank God...

leunig

Good heavens,
what happened
to you?

I shopped
'til I dropped.

But where is
your shopping?
I see no
parcels.

I dropped before I
got to the shops. I saw
the shops and fell down
in despair. I was struck
down by a great sense of ruin
and futility: a vision of ugliness;
of stupidity and vanity and a
world enslaved by its lazy,
wicked ways and its pompous
appetites.

It sounds like
you've had a
spiritual experience;
perhaps a retail or
shopping
centre
epiphany.

I blacked out
and saw the star
of Bethlehem right
here in the car park.

And did
you see the
little baby
sleeping?

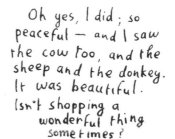

Oh yes, I did; so
peaceful — and I saw
the cow too, and the
sheep and the donkey.
It was beautiful.
Isn't shopping a
wonderful thing
sometimes?

Leunig

... and beneath the star there is a lowly shop and in the shop you will find a great bargain lying on a table...

Leunig

Zucchinis are like
people.

Yet in some ways
Zucchinis are not like
people. For instance, they
are peaceful and reliable
and content— in the main.

There are a lot of them
and they look good but
are they very interesting?
Maybe not.

They are good listeners.
They are trustworthy.
They seem to have an
attitude of "live and
let live".

And really, how many do
you want in your life?
Not many probably.

They would make excellent
friends were it not for
the fact that they are ...
ZUCCHINIS.

Leunig

A GLOOM

A gloom of one's own,
A picture or two,
A chair by the window,
A sad little view
Of yourself passing by
In the street all alone;
What a wonderful thing
Is a gloom of one's own

Leunig

MORE TO LIFE

An angel came and landed on the shed,
The little shed wherein my life is kept,
"There's more to life than this", the angel said.
We looked into each other's eyes and wept.

I hurried back inside and shut the door,
And all surrounded by the life I love
I lay there weeping on the concrete floor.
And heard the angel weeping up above.

Leunig

You people really
should keep up with
the news — it says
here that one in
four people suffer
from depression.

leunig

No sooner do you arrive than it's time to leave.

How beautiful it is.
How glorious. Yet it's
nearly time to go...
So you take it in,
you take it in...

You move towards the
open door and the silent
night beyond...
the few bright stars...
a deep breath...
and it really is time
to go.

... and you gather a few
small souvenirs: some
leaves... lavender,
rosemary, eucalyptus.
A few small pebbles
A few small secrets
A look you received
Nine little notes of music...
and then... it's time to go.

No sooner does it all
begin to make sense;
does it start to come
true; does it all open
up; do you begin to see;
does it enter into
your heart...

.. No sooner do you arrive
than it's time to leave.
Yes, it's the truth... and...
...and then you will have
passed through it ___ and
with mysterious consequence
it will have passed
through you.

Leunig

We must make do with scraps...

Little scraps of
peace and quiet.
Hope, conversation, handshakes
— all in dribs and drabs.

A few crumbs of fun
A tiny flake of beauty.
One teaspoon of enthusiasm.

A snippet of eye contact.
A snippet of hospitality.
A snippet of patience.

Off-cuts of each other
A skerrick of
   community...
A bit of a kiss.

A shred of honor.
A wisp of good humor.
A sample of compassion.

Leftovers, oddments,
remnants of the glorious
situation.
A fragment of God.
Not much really.
Sorry. Time's up.

Leunig

War Against Terror — the logo.

Here is the logo.

Here is the T-shirt

Here is the fragrance

Here is the shoulderbag.

Here is the store
There are the customers
There is the merchandise

PLUS
The CARD
The SHAREHOLDERS
and...
The LIFESTYLE

Leunig

Mr War
has been released
and is billeted
at our house.

He stands in
the corner and
stares at us while
we eat our dinner.
It's difficult to talk
or relax. He has
a nasty smell.

The next morning
the smell is right through
the house but we can't
see Mr War anywhere.
The heater won't
work. A picture has
fallen off the wall.

When we go to bed
Mr War stands in
the dark hallway
and we hear his
strange hard irregular
breathing all night.

It doesn't feel like
home any more. We
hear a strange rubbing
rasping noise up in
the ceiling. Everyone
feels a bit miserable
and uneasy.

We find Mr War's
boots and trousers
in the fridge. There
is a loud thumping
sound in the bathroom.
We don't know how
long Mr War is staying.

Leunig

... can you imagine if something like this was to fall into the wrong hands ?
leunig

Mr War, our unwanted, uninvited house guest shows no sign of leaving. What a morbid presence.

He is having a strange disturbing effect on our home. We are bickering a lot. Relationships are troubled.

Mr War has a huge, seething intensity but offers no meaning or sense. From the darkness of the next room he will suddenly cry out something like "BANG!" in a violently loud, ugly and demented voice.

Then silence. Later, a short snuffling laugh, a low growl, the quick squeaking of leather in the dark. A squalid disillusioning sense of shame, loneliness and confusion fills the home.

Yesterday Mr War left photographs in odd, prominent places all through the house; sordid sickening pictures of cruelty, savagery, blood and death.

We were shaken and distressed and deeply saddened. "BANG!" cried Mr War from the blackness of his room. And then his horrible snuffling.

leunig

The Warlords of Suburbia

The warlords of suburbia
Sitting on their couches
With lots of ammunition
In their pouches

"Death to the enemy!"
Is the warlord's cry.
And
"I think I'll have another
lovely piece of pie"

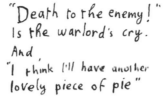

"Take his life!" mumbles
the warlord to himself,
"He's an evil swine!
Why should he have it?
I didn't have mine"

From the tiny balcony
That overlooks the neighbor's
pool
The warlord of suburbia dreams
of a concrete busting bomb —
And begins to drool

"Free the Arab women
from the veil!"
Says the warlord to
his wife,
Thinking how she'd
benefit
From the plastic surgeon's
Knife

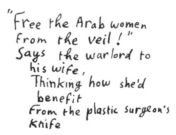

The warlord of suburbia
Totters off to bed
And lies there wondering
About being dead.

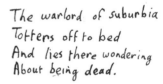

Leunig

SMOG TRAGEDY. Dead angels found in city park at dawn.

leunig

Letter from the REAL World.

" ... our community is holding a series of fundraisers to support the forthcoming military strike against the enemy.

We are sponsoring a landmine. The Defence Department has sent us a photograph of it. The photo is displayed on the noticeboard at the local supermarket. It's a nice beige colour.

Several cake stalls and a lamington drive have been conducted with great success.

Our landmine has the serial number:- DD-22BV1782/01 but we have named it "Bubby" because somebody described it jokingly as "an ankle biter."

A carwash and sausage sizzle will be held on Saturday at the scout hall to coincide with a walkathon. Let's hope it's a nice day.

SAUSAGE + BREAD + SAUCE $1.50

We will receive reports of Bubby's progress and be informed of any sudden developments.

BUBBY

CARE FOR BUBBY

Leunig

We are gathered
here to witness the
marriage of Fiona and Simon...

... Simon — do you
accept that you are
a complete jerk?

I do.

And do you, Fiona,
accept that you are
an absolute bitch?

I do.

I now declare
you married in
the true sense.
CONGRATULATIONS!

What a
beautiful
ceremony.

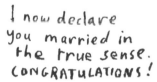

leunig

A BRIEF HISTORY OF HUMANS

Humans evolved from the primordial slime.

Eventually they established a sophisticated, technological slime...

...in which they live and work hard for shut-up money.

Sometimes the system breaks down, the power fails and love pops up, just like that!

leunig

UPON THE SAGGING MATTRESS

Upon the sagging mattress known as life
The weary husband lays down with his wife
To feel the nasty shapes and awful lumps;
To get no rest, to only get the grumps.
And yet upon this drooping bag of woe
They close their eyes and sometimes have a go
At fantasising sweeter, better things:
A life with good support and inner springs.

Distinguished Crying Cross.
FOR THOSE WHO HAVE REALLY WEPT.

Conspicuous Brevity Medal
FOR THOSE WHO DIDN'T GO ON AND ON AND ON.

Meritorious Thinking Medal
FOR THOSE WHO HAD SOME GOOD THOUGHTS.

THE Ordinary Star.
FOR THOSE WHO JUST MUDDLED ALONG AND DIDN'T LEAVE TOO MUCH MESS.

The Order of the Whoop.
For those who got away from the nonsense.

GENERAL VICTORY MEDAL.
For anybody who wants it and feels they deserve it.

Leunig

why do telephone cords twist?

why do telephone
cords twist?

Well actually, they
don't twist at all
They stay normal.

It is we who twist.
It is the world that
becomes twisted...

...A little more
each day. The telephone
cord is where it shows up.
But it's WE who are twisting!

IT is us.

Leunig

The Festival of Something or Other. OFFICIAL PROGRAMME

Welcome to the Festival of something or other. The GRAND OPENING DINNER WILL BE HELD SOMEWHERE AND WILL COMMENCE WHENEVER.

At some stage somebody will conduct a workshop some place about something or other.

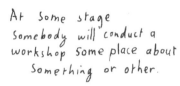

Someone or other will be the special star guest or whatever.

At some point somewhere there will be a debate or some such, between whoever turns up about anything. And why not?!

That will last for as long as it takes and then whatever happens happens — etc. etc.

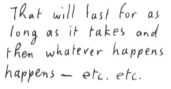

Something or other will continue for the next three days or so and then, who knows? WHATEVER!

Leunig

THE great DIVIDE ――― The HAVES and the HAVE - NOTS

THOSE who HAVE a twinkle in their eye.

Those who HAVE NOT got a twinkle in their eye.

Those who have sung in the moonlight in a forest glade with tears of happiness upon their cheeks.

THOSE WHO HAVE NOT.

THOSE WHO HAVE RUN OFF with the GIPSIES AND DANCED RAPTUROUSLY And FEASTED AND SLEPT IN THEIR ARMS and still have sweet memory OF IT.

THOSE WHO HAVE NOT.

AND JUST REPEATING, Those who HAVE a twinkle in their eye.

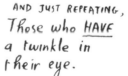

Those who HAVE NOT

Leunig

Who is that tragic figure
following at your heels?

... that forlorn
wretch hovering and
fidgeting around your
footsteps?

... that doubt-stricken
casualty who lies gasping
and snuffling under your
bed at
night?

... that pained
creature stumbling
confusedly in your wake?

... that mocking sniggering
ravenous, envious beast who
perches in a tree in the park
peering at you as you pass
below. Who is that?
who is it?

Could it be... ?
Could it possibly be...?
Oh dear! It is! YES...
It's... it's... No, surely not.
It couldn't be. BUT IT IS
YES IT IS...
IT'S... IT'S
THE OTHER YOU!

Leunig

Telephone sex is one of the great blessings and benefits of modern life which can too easily be taken for granted...

...Or those who had to manage with morse code as they sat hunched at lonely desks, tapping away with one finger at a clicking, mechanical key.

... So let us spare a thought for our forebears who had to do it by semaphore — waving signal flags while perched on rocky, windswept hilltops or barren, icy crags.

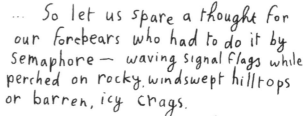

Or the carrier pigeon people — what gifted and dedicated people they were; and such effective and economical writers — just a few well-chosen words scrawled on a cigarette paper and wrapped around a pigeon's leg. Amazing!

Leunig

So how do we
face the future?

IT IS DIFFICULT
BECAUSE THE FUTURE
CREEPS UP FROM BEHIND
NO MATTER WHICH
WAY YOU'RE
FACING.

AND IT FALLS OUT
OF THE SKY TOO AND
LANDS ON YOUR HEAD.

IT ALSO COMES OUT
OF THE GROUND AND
CRAWLS UP YOUR LEG.

In that case we'll do
somersaults and spin
around in circles and
generally roll
about!

VERY
WISE...

Leun·

How can
I help
?

I'd like
some
humility
please.

Humility.
Certainly !
Just the
one packet ?

There's six
cartons out
in the storeroom.
I'll do you a
special price
on the six.

Actually,
I was just
wondering ;
can I get it
in bulk ?

What about
a carton?
That's ten
packets.
It's cheaper.

Maybe a
few cartons
would be a
good idea.

You mean
by the truckload?
Sure! How many
truckloads do
you want?

How big
are the
trucks?

They range
from ordinary
tip trucks right
up to huge
road trains.
Whatever you
like.

Oh, by the
way, I'd
like some
simplicity too.
What types of
simplicity
have
you
got?

leunig

Doctor, I'm going through a huge change of life...
And...?
...and I'm not sure whether I'm going mad or...
or...?
... or whether I'm going sane.
Is there any pain ?
There is the agonising pain of an almost unbearable anguish...
You're going sane...
Leunig

Small Towns

There is a little town called Me
Where things aren't what they used to be
And nearby is the town of You
Which is getting tired too.

But we can take the morning bus
And travel to the town of Us;
A larger, louder place with bells;
With parks and schools and wishing wells;
Churches, restaurants and shops;
Potatoes, pumpkin, peas and chops;
Some ginger sponge, a cup of tea,
Then back again to You and Me.

You.   Me.

BUS STOP

THE RAGING RIVER

HAPPY VALLEY

THE DARK FOREST

THE GREAT MOUNTAIN

TRUE NORTH

Us.

Leunig

La-La Land.

I want to go to La-La Land
And have a holiday;
In La-La Land they'll understand
The thing I have to say.

I'll rent the little wonky shack
That overlooks the bay
And wait until it all comes back:
This thing I have to say.

And then one night I'll bow my head
While strolling on the sand
And say the thing that must be said
Out loud in La-La Land.

leunig

Life is _Offensive_ and refuses to apologise.

The rose bush — an arch conservative with cruel thorns.

DEATH — the right-wing radical.

The heartless, dull bureaucracy of _time_.

The cat?
The cat is probably a monarchist!

The dog — a naked opportunist; a moral vacuum; an uneducated, pleasure-driven philistine.

And the moon — so aloof, so cold so full of itself.

Leunig

The journey between waking up in the morning and the first cup of tea is precarious and immensely sad. It requires courage.

The journey from the first cup of tea to the first encounter with the dog is full of hope and pleasure.

The journey from the desk to the first daydream is pleasant, winding and mysterious.

The journey from the dog
to the desk is difficult,
serious and erratic.

The journey from the
daydream back to the
desk is bleak, uncomfortable
and dispiriting — yet heroic
all the same.

And so the various journeys
continue— hundreds of them,
until the great circumnavigation
reaches its finale: the
glorious, triumphant journey
between the feet leaving
the floor and the head
arriving on the pillow.

Leunig

In a mad modern world an old-fashioned sanity can be an embarrassment and a liability.

So slow.
So cumbersome.
Constant maintenance.
Spare parts are difficult to find.

And even if you've got one in working order, what can you do with it? Not much it seems.

There's little call for it these days, and no wonder, it's GENERAL INCOMPATIBILITY has caused it to become AN INCONVENIENCE!

Enthusiasts keep on with it, just for the sheer pleasure. Some of them dream of a revival.

They think it could be worth something one day. That's a FORLORN HOPE.

Leunig

He woke up
feeling
inappropriate

Some inappropriate
thoughts entered
his mind

He said
something
inappropriate
to his wife

He put on some
inappropriate
clothing

And went out
to walk in an
inappropriate
place

How inappropriate
the world
seemed. A big
inappropriate
smile spread
across his face

leunig

The Wine Regions of our House.

Most of the truly great wines have been produced from the <u>Pantry</u>, which is a cool climate region.

The fridge produces mainly white wines and the quality is mostly quite o.k.

Very drinkable wines have been produced from under the front seat of the car.

The shed is a warmer region but consistently produces some wonderful surprises.

A high-altitude region is the top of the bookshelf and perfectly magnificent wines can be found there. The letter box also produces the odd excellent bottle.

These days, wines are being produced from all sorts of unlikely and improbable places. Modern life is certainly creating some fascinating surprises.

leunig

The pie of life
Is hurled into your face
Every day
But that is no disgrace.

A life worth living
Gets splattered on your shirt —
And though you're shocked
And rather deeply hurt;
These pies of life
Which fly out of the blue:
You're made for them
And they were made for you.

leunig

Doctor I've got a feeling.

You poor thing, tell me all about it.

It's a little pang of lonely sorrow. Do you think it's a personality disorder? Can it be painlessly removed?

It's affecting my eyes. They've developed a sad, disillusioned, exiled, abandoned, look.

It could
be LHS;
Live Human
Syndrome.

And tell
me, do you
believe in the
war against
terror?

No I don't.
And I don't believe
in the great global
promise or the boom
economy or
supermarkets or
major events
or talkback radio
or opinion polls
or...

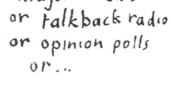

That's it.
You've
got it,
You've
got
LHS...

Leunig

Summer Diary

Yesterday, normality was supposed to return but it didn't.

..."it's not coming back," said a man in the street, "...It's all finished; kaput!"

"They've stopped making it," said the lady in the shop, "...discontinued! people weren't using it, too slow!"

"There was no such thing as normality," said a smart looking fellow, "it was all a bloody lie." He was so sure of himself.

I believed in it, although I couldn't really prove it existed — nor could I describe it very well...

... except to say that it seemed to hold everything together more or less.
Anyway I'm going to miss normality for the time being but I'm not giving up hope.
I need it.

Leunig

SUMMER diary

Yesterday I read the newspaper.

It sucked the life out of me.

A feeling of gloomy bitterness and futility dragged me to the floor.

The dog came and began to lick my face.

After about five minutes of licking, hope started to return to my body;

... not much, but enough for me to be able to slowly sit up and say, "good dog."

Leunig

summer diary

yesterday I went to the cricket.

There it was, just sitting on the ground, all shiny and black.

I like watching the cricket — the troubles of the world fade from my thoughts — everything seems so civilized.

I sit and watch and the day passes gently. Life seems worth living. I feel contented.

Some find the cricket boring but not me. I love it when he crawls into a crack in the ground and starts to sing.

His song is so beautiful, so atmospheric, so mysterious. I love listening to the cricket, particularly on a warm summer's night after a little rain.

Leunig

our way of life is
being threatened by
a dark force.

we must defend our
way of life.

WHAT IS THIS
DARK FORCE WHICH
THREATENS OUR WAY
OF LIFE ?

it's our way
of life...

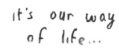

Leunig

THAT'S ONE
SMALL STEP
FOR MAN...

...and that's
another small
step for man...

...That's a
Small to
average
size step...

...that's a
dreary half-
hearted step;
very average...

that's
another
one... and
another...
and
another...
and
another...
...that's a
bit smaller
than average...
...that's another...

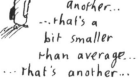

Leunig

They were Australians.
He was a republican.
She was a monarchist.

They fell in love.
They got married.

They had two
beautiful children;

One was an anarchist;
The other was a fascist

The household operated
as an anarchistic,
fascist, republican
monarchy.

At the end of the day
they called the system
"our joint", or "our place", and
sometimes "home, sweet home".

leunig

He sat on his chair and thought "I'm sitting on an icon; the chair, in its functional simplicity, is truly a great icon."

He sipped his tea and thought "A cup of tea is a great icon also."

And out there, through the window, the world was full of icons. "The world is one big icon" he thought.

He looked out the window and thought, "What a wonderful icon is the common domestic window."

And then he thought, "I used to be ironic and laconic but now I'm.... ...I'm ICONIC!

"◎#✱!!", he said to himself; and no sooner had the word left his lips than he realised what a great icon it was — this amazing word.

Leunig

To be on the safe side
I took out the fine-tooth
comb of retrospection to
run it through my life—

To comb out all
the dark dirty bits
of my history; the
silly messy naughty
mistakes

I had now turned
myself into a piece
of HUMAN CONFECTIONERY;
what a SUCCESS!

After combing furiously
for several hours I had
gotten rid of all the
nasty little lumps.

I had attained
MARSHMALLOWDOM
the highest, most
attractive and
perfect state of
being and the
epitome of
GETTING IT RIGHT.

I was also
stuck to the chair,
but more about
that later...

Leunig

HUSHED SPECTATORS WATCHING THE FINISH OF THE MAVIS CUP.

VARIOUS LAPTOPS

IRONING BOARD

PASTA MAKER

SHRINE

BUTTERFLY COLLECTION

PIPE ORGAN

FLOWER PRESS

Leunig

*One of the most AMAZING and SIGNIFICANT events of the twentieth century took place on a creaking bed in a small hut on a remote WINDSWEPT HILLSIDE in rural Australia many years ago...

To this day nobody has ever revealed what happened !

Leunig

... What's going to become of us all...?
DISASTER, WOE AND ALL DYSFUNCTIONS GREAT AND SMALL
We'll probably become who we really are...
... a grisly but hopeful thought
Leunig

His world had changed since the evil terrorist had entered, so cunningly, into his body while he slept.

Now it was living _inside_ him; secretly plotting his downfall and he couldn't locate it or flush it out.

Maybe it was in his skull — snipping all the little wires and tampering with his brain chemistry...

Where was it hiding? In his
stomach? In his heart? Perhaps
the terrorist was lurking in the
darkness of his bowels.

...which might cause him to
lose control and do something
terrible. Heaven forbid!

But worse still, the terrorist could
cause his hair to fall out, his
flesh to sag and wither and
his entire body to age and weaken;
what a vile atrocity.
   The evil one is everywhere; is
anything. Death to the evil one,
not to us. Heaven forbid!

Leunig

I'm sorry about this but all the polls and all the talkback are saying I've got to crucify you...
Leunig

Hey Loser!
Get a life!

just my
lousy luck.
I'll take
the size
ten.

A LOOSE
LIFE IS
MORE FUN
THAN A
TIGHT ONE.

... I think I'm a size Four.

WE'VE ONLY GOT SIZE TEN AND SIZE TWO.

My grandmother made her own life. It looked quite plain but it fitted her beautifully...

AH YES. THE GOOD OLD DAYS. WE'VE ONLY GOT A PURPLE ONE IN SIZE TEN.

What colour is the size two?

SIZE TWO IS PURPLE WITH THE ORANGE AND BROWN STRIPES... VERY SMART.

Leunig

...and who is that happy
Soul beside you, so
unabashed, holding that
great big bunch of flowers;

...holding your arm and
singing that trashy
song you love in
secret;

Who is that?
Who is that tickling
the palm of your hand
and whispering in your
ear "Yes!...go on; I dare you"?

... the trashy song that brings you to a halt; brings you to your knees; brings you to your precious tears of happiness. ?

Who is it that clears your mess while you sleep; Who waits calmly for your awakening; who loves you from afar ?

Could it be ?
Could it possibly be ?
YES, it IS.
OF COURSE IT IS. it's...
THE OTHER YOU!

Leunig

They tapped his phone. They heard his conversation.

He was having one of those fantasy chats with an anonymous woman; Five dollars per minute.

" Love your fellow creatures," she continued, "open your heart to nature's beautiful truth; honour it with courage wisdom and tenderness, and be of good cheer."

" Patience, simplicity, compassion," she said to him, " these are the great treasures."

"Yes Yes YES!", he moaned blissfully as he heard the forbidden words.

They heard it all. They recorded everything. And now he was in BIG TROUBLE.

PRAYER

See him wandering alone.
The crowdless man.
He has no group.
He has no tribe.

He carries his identity
In his pocket.
His pocket
Has a hole in it.

His story
Has a hole in it.
His tragedy
Is not a tune
You can hum.

His suffering and sacrifice:
They have no handles.
His persecution
Has no logo,
No shrine
No yardstick.

His joy has no credentials.
His observations have
No fixed address.
There are no awards
Whatsoever.

His gaze and yearning
Are way outside the loop.
His pilgrimage,
Has lots of holes in it.
See him wandering alone
Beaming to himself!

Leunig

Moments of no consequence
Seem to make a lot of sense;
Like the gentle pitter patter
Of the things that do not matter
As I sit alone and stare;
Neither here and neither there.

O.K. DRIVER...
PULL
over...

WOULD YOU MIND
THINKING INTO THIS
BAG PLEASE

Hang on, I'll
just get the reading...
oh dear... you've had
one too many...
      haven't you...

You've
caught me
this time...

O.K.
I admit it. Yes.
...but you don't
blame me do
you...

No... but you
must be careful —
thinking too many
of those sad dreadful
thoughts about
    humanity...
    you could hurt
        yourself...
    or somebody
        else... now you
just go home and
sleep it off... o.k.

Leunig

THE ORIGIN AND MEANING OF TENNIS

Tennis was invented in Ely, Cambridgeshire, England in 1632 by Lord Tennis.

Lord Tennis suffered from melancholia and felt his sadness to be round in shape and located in his chest.

The eccentric Lord created a small leather ball to symbolically represent this sadness so that he could contemplate it more effectively.

He wondered if his sadness might leave him if he were to throw the ball away. So he threw it over the front fence.

The ball landed in the street in front of a passing minstrel who took a swipe at it with his lute and the ball hurtled back to the amazed Lord.

In great excitement the Lord took his own lute and belted the ball back into the street and the first "Tennis match" then took place with the "ball of melancholia". The deep symbolism of tennis still lives on to this very day.

Leunig

Last night I saw a gentle fool
Standing in the sea
Puffing at a little boat;
The good ship "Bumble Bee".

He puffed and blew into the sail
And as the sky grew pink
The "Bumble Bee" quite definitely
Began to slowly sink.

And then it sank and it was gone.
The air turned sweet and cool
The sea was gold and purple
All around the gentle fool.

leunig

The Empty Jeff Syndrome.

An empty Jeff came through the clouds
And hung there for a minute:
A vacuum in the shape of Jeff
With no Jeff in it!

"The empty Jeff, the empty Jeff!"
The people cried in awe,
All staring at the space where Jeff
Was very much no more.

Leunig

Ye Olde Sayeings of Journalism

YOU CAN MAKE A SILK PURSE OUT OF A SOW's EAR • Any port in a journalist (OR BRANDY) • If the cap fits, write about it • TO ERR IS JOURNALISM • Genius is the infinite capacity for taking • Fear the journalists bearing gifts • JOURNALISM IS THE GREAT LEVELLER • The squeaking journalist gets the grease • HE WHO PAYS THE JOURNALIST CALLS THE TUNE • The voice of the journalist is the voice of God • REVENGE IS JOURNALISM • All good things must be brought to an end • THE DRIVEL FINDS WORK FOR IDLE JOURNALISTS TO DO • Always the journalist, never the bride • Imitation is the sincerest form of journalism • Stolen stories are sweet • A LITTLE JOURNALIST IS A DANGEROUS THING • You can make a sow's ear out of a silk purse • Whom the Gods would destroy they first make journalists • JOURNALISM IN ALL THINGS • Write nothing of what you hear and only half of what you see • JOURNALISM IS THE MOTHER OF INVENTION • Between two journalists one falls to the ground • THE DARKEST HOUR IS JUST BEFORE THE JOURNALIST • Leunig

THIS WEEK'S TOP TEN BEST SELLING NEWSPAPERS, MAGAZINES, PERIODICALS, JOURNALS

Braying Twit

- MEDIA
- DESIGN
- TRAVEL
- ART

CRUDE LUNGE

- STYLE
- ENTERTAINMENT
- DESIGN
- ART

FATUOUS CLAPTRAP INCORPORATING "SMARTALEC DRIVEL"

- MEDIA
- DESIGN
- LIVING
- ART

INANE FOP MONTHLY

- FILM
- STYLE
- TRAVEL
- DESIGN

SHALLOW GUFF MONTHLY

- FILM
- STYLE
- TECHNO FASHION
- ART

Loudmouth Perspectives

- MEDIA
- LIVING
- STYLE
- TECHNO DESIGN

Prattling Dingbat

- TECHNO FASHION
- FILM
- LIVING
- MEDIA

PUSHY TWADDLE WEEKLY

- ART
- STYLE
- ENTERTAINMENT
- MEDIA

SCREECHING NINNY BULLETIN

- STYLE
- ENTERTAINMENT
- ART
- MEDIA

THE DAILY IDIOT

- STYLE
- DESIGN
- MEDIA
- ART

Leunig

Are you getting <u>MORE</u> sausage or <u>LESS</u> sausage?

Are you getting a <u>LESS FREQUENT</u> sausage which is more pleasing?

Or are you getting a <u>different</u> sausage which is more exciting?

How do you measure prosperity and wellbeing? That which can be measured cannot be truly enjoyed.

leunig

DO YOU
THINK KEN'S
CONSTIPATION
WILL END
HAPPILY ?

The ending is
unimportant; what
matters most is
the sheer drama
of his difficult
and lonely
situation.

Leunig

I looked inside my heart and saw a ship
Sailing merrily upon a rip;
Moving blissfully against the tide:
"IRRELEVANCE" was written   on her side.

Her brightly colored sail,
her oars of gold
Her fiddler,
her navigator bold;
"God be with you
one and all" I cried.
"IRRELEVANCE" was written
on her side.

IRRELEVANCE

Leunig

The politicians
don't like listening
to the people.

The people don't
like listening to
the politicians.

The politicians don't
like listening to
each other.
Except for gossip.

The people don't
like listening to
each other.
Except for gossip,

Listening can
be difficult.

Eavesdropping and
overhearing: these
things are FREE, EXCITING
and lots of FUN, and therefore
more practical and POPULAR
than
LISTENING.

Leunig

THE LAST FLIGHT OF THE LONELY PASSION

The last flight of the "Lonely Passion",
Our one remaining plane,
Took off late on Sunday night
And was never seen again.

It is said, amongst a host of other things,
That there were various malfunctions in the wings;
In fact a very large collection.
The fact is, the wings were _made_ of imperfection.

And yet such beautiful, functional things:
Imperfections carefully woven into wings;
Failings great, but mostly medium to small,
But something strangely uplifting in every fall.
You see, it didn't fly
By means of a propeller or a rocket burning;
It rose into the heavens
By the pure boldness of its yearning!

And now our "Lonely Passion" is unaccounted for.
Maybe it strayed into the airspace or the headspace
of a wicked unforgiving war.
Or maybe in the night of all this fearful, sad and
bitter thinking.
Its little navigation light is somewhere blinking.

Leunig

The CHATTERING CLASSES

Chattering is one of life's natural pleasures. All healthy creatures do it with joyous abandon.

There are those, however, who have trouble and need to attend chattering classes to receive help and to find relief.

In the chattering classes they learn to unravel their inhibitions, to relax and flow and to discover the hidden treasure of their ordinary, natural, convivial chatter.

Unfortunately there are some who are beyond help and they usually drop out of the chattering classes in a frustrated, miserable and embittered condition whereupon they sometimes attempt to make a virtue of their failure and dysfunction.

In such places as newspaper columns they will attack and condemn the chattering classes in a petulant, mean spirited and unseemly manner. This is wowserism in all its futility and as such is actually quite entertaining in a perverse way.

But chattering is universal good fun. It is a vivacious, persistent and indestructible human impulse. Chattering classes are helpful, enjoyable and hugely successful. Nattering is also lots of fun but more about that later.

Leunig

Modern Stupid

It's much easier to go stupid these days than in previous times.

Now we can do it faster and with more comfort and convenience thanks to modern methods and technology.

Back in the old days they had to do it all by hand. It was sheer drudgery.

You can easily fit it into a busy life. It's available to everybody; right there at your fingertips.

Leunig

Us.

Last night while looking at the sky
I saw a little planet die
It died and fell without a fuss
I wondered whether it was us —
Or part of us that I had seen
Disintegrate. It could have been.

Leunig

Autumn Poem

The pen is mightier than the gourd
But the gourd is more contented
And beautiful and self-assured;
The pen is more demented.
It craves to make its mark and then
It dreads to be ignored.
I want to be less of a pen
And be more of a gourd.

leunig

The little clip
That seals the bread
Lost its grip
Inside his head

The bread spilled out
Into his life
He gave a shout
He found a knife

He found some cheese
And then some ham,
Some lettuce leaves
And pickle jam

The wine appeared
He took a sip,
And thought, "How weird:
The little clip"

Leunig

Oh great and glorious God,
almighty powerful father
of heaven and earth...

... grant us your everlasting
strength and wisdom
in our fight against
evil...

O.K.
I grant it
to you..
...

EH !
Who are you?

I'm God.

You can't be God,
you're too small.

sorry to
disappoint you
but I am
God.

You're so little !
This is totally
RIDICULOUS !

You're so big.
It's completely
mad.

Leunig

Happiness   is   just   a   little   thing

Humans   mostly   are   too   large   for   it.
If you   cannot   feel   the joy of   spring;

Shrink
                        yourself   and   maybe   then   you'll   fit.

Leunig

$\oint$ UNDERPANTS WHICH HAVE, IN WINTER, SAGGED   (a hymn for spring)

Underpants which have, in winter, sagged
And fallen into darkness and despond
Shall from their shame and loneliness be dragged
And laid upon the fern's emerging frond
The frond shall gently rise to greet the Spring,
Above the flowers, into the sun fantastic,
Where birds in praise of underpants shall sing
And life will be restored to old elastic

Leunig

Artist, artist in your garret
With your pussy cat and parrot,
Why are you not taking part
In the festival of art?

Here's the reason I'm not part
Of the festival of art:
I am feasting in my garret
With my pussy cat and parrot.

leunig

Another Little Mystery

He used to talk to himself but not any more; now he whispered to himself — and quite frequently too.

One day he stopped in his tracks: "SPEAK UP OR SHUT UP AND forever hold your peace!", he cried to himself in desperation.

Wherever he went the whispering went with him — the trouble was, he couldn't quite hear what he was whispering; it was _so_ soft.

After that the whispering stopped and never returned. He became stricken with a forlorn sense that a huge and vital revelation had been lost to him forever.

Soft, yet it sounded very much in earnest — as if it were an important secret or a dire warning — but he just couldn't quite hear what it _was_.

If only he'd gone somewhere still and quiet and slow and had just listened patiently and been able to hear. If only...

Leunig

What's the use of this little hand;
What's the use of this little eye;
What's the use of this little mouth
When all the world is broken?

Make a cake with this little hand;
Make a tear with this little eye;
Make a word with this little mouth
When all the world is broken

Leunig

Rustle Crow

Rustle crow, rustle crow,
How you make the cockles glow
As you rustle to and fro
In my lonely garden

And I know, and I know
It's a blessing you bestow
As you rustle soft and low
In my lonely garden.

It is so, it is so,
All the world is full of woe,
Yet the angels come and go
In my lonely garden.

oh dear,
we're doomed;
the world's
getting hotter.

yes but it's getting
harder too; so it doesn't
feel the heat so much

...and it's getting faster too
which creates a bit of a
turbulent breeze which
cools things down a bit...

...and also, it's getting
madder which means
nobody cares or notices
very much... so
everything's
normal
and quite
o.k.

Leunig

Magpie, magpie dive on me
Swoop down from your holy tree
As I pass the flower bed
Stick your beak into my head

Magpie, magpie make a hole
Through my head into my soul.
As I pass beneath the sun
Bring my troubled head undone

Magpie, magpie it is spring
Is my soul a happy thing?
As I pass around the tree,
Make a hole so you can see.

What ruined your life?
I was abused by a priest when I was a child.
What happened?
He told me to be forgiving and humble and not to talk bullshit...
And what's the problem with that?
The problem is that I took him seriously.
He took advantage of your innocence!
RUINED MY LIFE... !!
...I could have been the treasurer or something...
Leunig

The strain of being acceptable begins to take its mysterious toll. You can see it in the eyes.

All those "being acceptable" classes; the books, the videos — "HOW TO BE ACCEPTABLE" — all those rules and exercises.

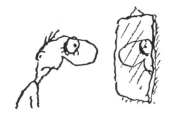

And worse still, much worse, the "BEING ATTRACTIVE" project : all that desperate running; the exhausting vigilance; the soul-destroying labour.

Yes...

The stress of the constant "BEING ACCEPTABLE" competitions, the grinding performances, the tedium of practice, the cold discipline etc, etc.

But wait! Even worse; more hideous and painful the disgraceful, disgusting activity known as, "ACTING NORMAL" Oh, yes.

That as well!

Dear, oh dear, oh dear! ... the terrible wear and tear, the sheer futility, the tragic waste, the pathetic shame etc. etc. etc.

Leunig

GOOD MORNING
I saw a film called... "Good Morning".
I'M JUST WISHING YOU GOOD MORNING.
I saw a film called "WISHING YOU."
HOLY HELL.
HOW BIZARRE.
"HOLY HELL" is an Italian art movie I saw it.
... and "BIZARRE" was a documentary film made in London in the sixties.
Also, the expression on your face reminds me of somebody in a Woody Allen film.
Hey, you run just like the guy in "Chariots of Fire". Hang on. Now you're running like Peter O'Toole in "Lawrence of Arabia" when he was on top of the train after the massacre scene.
Leunig

What is GLOBALISATION?

...That's when a woman in New York...

... a man in Hobart...

... a child in Oslo

...a canary in Milan

... an old lady in Peru, a dolphin off the coast of Madagascar...

...all share the same anxiety and the same despair for the same reason at the same time.

Leunig

A magnificent man casting seeds in the direction of a wonderful woman.

Leunig

REJOICE!

The people in your world (including you)
They are your humble ration in this life
This flakey, raggle taggle, motley crew;
Your nasty husband and your silly wife.

Your lovely wife, your darling husband too;
Your happy neighbor sobbing on all fours;
Oh, the sweet and feeble things they do;
You are theirs, alas, and they are yours.

And you are yours as well and you are you
And all that's left of you (your dwindling passion)
Rejoice, rejoice whatever else you do
Rejoice and nibble sweetly on your ration.

leunig

BILLY the rabbit
is dead.

He died in his cage
On a cool afternoon
With Sarah the guinea pig
There by his side.

"Billy", she cried
And everything broke
As she broke down and
gathered up Sarah
And walked through the rain
Sobbing, "Billy, poor Billy
is dead."

The girl who had named him
And cuddled him joyfully
Came home from school and discovered
him
Lying there pitifully, beautifully;
Billy the rabbit
   uncuddled and dead.

It's evening
And Billy is lying in state
on the verandah;
All speckled with petals,
Surrounded by freshly picked
grasses and flowers;
In a fruit box
With one little wobbly candle
Casting some light on a
note at his feet.

"DEAR BILLY I COTDT
KEEP CRYING WHEN YOU
DIED I AM SO SORRY FOR
SARIR AND YOU
         FROM ...."
And there was her name
And a drawing of Billy all smiling
Signed with new mystery and
meaning:
The name of the girl
Who had come home to find
That Billy, her rabbit was dead.

leunig

YEARNING APHORISMS

This person is yearning
It's not obvious.

Yearning is an
exquisitely private or
secret condition.

What is yearned
is true.
To yearn is to see.

Yearning is a well-tended
hope which has ripened
slowly into a sweet,
sensuous prayer.

Yearning is the natural remedy for discontent, agitation, non-specific grievance, prickly sensibility and similar modern ailments.

Yearning brings poise to the imagination, a pleasant momentum to consciousness and an angel who plays a lute which drowns out the noise of the traffic.

Yearning lifts you up out of the courtroom; away from the judge, the police, the lawyers and the witnesses against you; it raises you out through the window and up into the sunshine and the beautiful blue sky.

leunig

Anyone can get a life.
Anyone can lose it
But who will dare to inhabit the thing
And <u>use</u> it?

A lived in life
  will soon get loose
  and worn
  From use and feeling;
Countless tiny scratches:
The shine goes off.
It's very unappealing!

Another broken sleep.
A dream collapses.
A quick repair. It's worth a try.
A scrap of string from the soul.
Perhaps a battered grin
  will fill the hole —
Or just a sigh.

Dirt builds up,
A load of muck and grit
A part of you gets lost —
A hope, a philosophy
Or a love that doesn't fit.

Flakes and cracks!
A major idea buckles badly
A makeshift support is
Invoked quickly.
A tired old joke could
hide the dint.
Or be a wedge, or a patch
or a splint...
Truly sweetly, sadly.

And yet it works and lives!
It all still goes. It forgives.
It's a miracle!
Worn in, bashed in, cried in,
And the great thing —
A lived in life
Can be happily died in.

Leunig

ANNOUNCEMENT.

A very limited period
of time is coming when
no festival, celebration or
major event will be making
a claim upon your existence.

Perhaps it could be called
"ordinary time" or "peace"
or "ordinary life". It has
no official name. It may
not last very long.

And there will be no
logo, no poster, no slogan.
There will be the dripping
of the tap, the ticking of
the clock and the coming and
going of plain and ordinary
things.

There will be no fireworks
nor will there be a release
of doves or balloons; nor
will there be "special offers"
of any kind. and no
"information hot line".

Perhaps you will also hear a
bird sing or a spoon move in
a bowl or a person whistling
over the back fence or the
sound of pruning secateurs
on a rose bush. Who knows.

There will be no
media coverage; no commentary
or analysis. It will all pass
unremarked upon.
Are you ready?

Leunig

THE PAST

THE FUTURE

THE PASTURE